# Jewish Americans

# *Our* CULTURAL HERITAGE

SPIRIT
of America®

# *Jewish*AMERICANS

## By Pam Rosenberg

Content Adviser: James La Forest, Judaica Librarian, Chicago, Illinois

The Child's World®
Chanhassen, Minnesota

10

# *Jewish*AMERICANS

**Published in the United States of America by The Child's World®**
P.O. Box 326 • Chanhassen, MN 55317-0326 • 800-599-READ • www.childsworld.com

*Acknowledgments*

The Child's World®: Mary Berendes, Publishing Director

Editorial Directions, Inc.: E. Russell Primm, Editorial Director and Line Editor; Katie Marsico, Assistant Editor; Matthew Messbarger, Editorial Assistant; Susan Hindman, Copy Editor; Susan Ashley, Proofreader; Julie Zaveloff, Chris Simms, and Peter Garnham, Fact Checkers; Tim Griffin/IndexServ, Indexer; Dawn Friedman, Photo Researcher; Linda S. Koutris, Photo Selector

The Design Lab: Kathleen Petelinsek, Art Direction; Kari Thornborough, Page Production

*Photos*

Cover/frontispiece: A group of Jewish immigrants, New York City, 1908.

Cover photographs ©: Corbis; Corbis; Richard T. Nowitz/Corbis.

Interior photographs ©: Bettmann/Corbis: 11, 14, 21, 23, 24; Corbis: 9 (Leonard de Selva), 10 (Nik Wheeler), 12 (Archivo Iconografico, S.A.), 17 (Rose Eichenbaum), 18 (Photo Collection Alexander Alland, Sr.), 19 (Lee Snider; Lee Snider), 25 (Mitchell Gerber), 28 (Reuters NewMedia Inc.); Getty Images/Hulton Archive: 15; Magnum Photos: 6 (Bruce Davidson) 16 (Bar Am Collection), 26 (Philippe Halsman).

*Library of Congress Cataloging-in-Publication Data*
Rosenberg, Pam.
  Jewish Americans / by Pam Rosenberg.
    p. cm. — (Our cultural heritage)
  Includes index.
  Contents: A scattered people—Coming to America—Becoming American—Famous Jewish Americans.
    ISBN 1-59296-181-9 (lib. bdg. : alk. paper)
  1. Jews—United States—Juvenile literature. {1. Jews—United States.} I. Title. II. Series.
  E184.J5R61958 2004
  973'.04924—dc22                                    2003018094

15       21       28

# Contents

# Chapter ONE

# A Scattered People

THE UNITED STATES IS A NATION OF IMMIGRANTS. Its citizens or their ancestors come from countries around the world. Jews are only one of the many ethnic groups living there. But, unlike other ethnic groups, Jews came to America from many different places. A common homeland is not what binds Jewish Americans together. It is, instead, a common religion and culture that make up their shared experience.

*The Eldridge Street Synagogue in New York City was built in 1887 as a place for Jews from Eastern Europe to worship. Through the years the synagogue, like many others, served not only as a house of worship but as a place for Jewish immigrants to find the help they needed to adapt to life in the United States.*

Judaism, the religion of the Jews, can be traced back to ancient times. It has its roots in the Bible stories of Abraham and Moses. In ancient times, the ancestors of the Jews settled in the region between Egypt and the Fertile Crescent, in a place called Canaan, centered in present-day Israel. They believed this land to be the holy land—their Promised Land—given to them by God.

In 586 B.C., the Jews lost their homeland. They were forced into exile in Babylonia, the land between the Tigris and Euphrates Rivers. They remained there for the next 50 years. Then King Cyrus, the Persian ruler, allowed them to return and rebuild their temple. The Jews stayed in their homeland for about 600 years. In A.D. 70, the Romans began forcing out the Jews again. Only a handful of Jews remained in the city of Jerusalem and other small communities nearby.

Most of the Jews settled in other parts of the Mediterranean region. Jewish communities developed in Spain, Italy, North Africa, and the part of present-day Turkey that is on the Asian continent. Over time, some moved further into Europe and settled in Germany. In all of these places, the Jews learned the languages of their new countries and learned the customs of their new neighbors. For centuries, many Jews made their living by trading—buying and selling goods to other

## Interesting Fact

▸ The city of Jerusalem is considered a holy city by Jews, Christians, and Muslims. For Jews, it is the center of their history, and they consider it to be the capital of Israel. Christians honor the city as the place where Jesus, whom they consider the Son of God, died and was resurrected. Muslims make pilgrimages to the city to visit the Dome of the Rock, built on the site where the Prophet Muhammad, the founder of Islam, is said to have ascended into heaven.

7

people. They were the middlemen in trade between different communities throughout the world. This meant that they worked with people who brought in goods from foreign locations and then resold them to merchants. The merchants then sold the goods to the public. But, even though they lived and worked freely with people from many parts of the world, most Jews never gave up their religious identity. They established Jewish communities within their new communities and maintained a sense of separateness.

This sense of separateness was important in maintaining their identity as Jews while living in places throughout the world. At times, they lived in great harmony with non-Jews in their new homelands. For instance, in Spain, under Muslim rulers, they enjoyed full membership in society and were able to practice their Jewish faith openly. But, in predominantly Christian countries, Jews were often persecuted. Although Jesus was a Jew, Christian religious leaders taught their followers that Jews were to blame for his death. Christians found it difficult to accept that the great majority of Jews stayed true to their religious beliefs instead of converting to Christianity. So, when times were bad, Jews were an easily identifiable group to blame. It was during one of these periods of persecution that Jews began their journey to America.

IN THE FINAL YEARS OF THE 11TH CENTURY, CHRISTIAN SOLDIERS FROM Europe set out for Jerusalem. Their goal was to take the city back from the Muslims who controlled it at the time. Along the way, these **Crusaders** murdered many Jews in Germany and parts of France, a region identified as *Ashkenaz* in the Jewish tradition. The majority of survivors fled to countries further east in Europe, settling in Poland, Russia, Lithuania, and Bohemia. Because they came from the region known as Ashkenaz, these Jews came to be called *Ashkenazim.* Over time, the Jews in eastern Europe were persecuted, so many Ashkenazim resettled in western Europe.

The Jews who had been living in Spain and Portugal settled elsewhere after the **Inquisition** of the late 15th century. They are known as *Sephardim,* or Spaniards. Many of the Sephardim were heavily involved in the business of trading. Most of them were better off financially than the Ashkenazim.

Because of differences in their history, the Ashkenazim and Sephardim developed their own distinct Jewish cultures and rituals. Today, more than 80 percent of Jews are descendants of the Ashkenazim. In Israel, however, the numbers of Ashkenazim and Sephardim are almost equal.

# Chapter Two

# Coming to America

JEWISH AMERICANS HAVE BEEN LIVING IN NORTH America since before the United States was born. They were among the first settlers to arrive from Europe.

Spain had been home to many Jews for centuries. In the 14th century, however, Christians began to drive the Muslim leaders out of the country. The

*The Alhambra Palace in Granada, Spain, probably dates back to the 13th century. It was used by Muslim rulers until the Christian king and queen of Spain took control of Granada in 1492.*

new Christian leaders, like Christians in other parts of the world, had little tolerance for the Jews. Hoping to avoid persecution and possibly death, many Jews outwardly converted to Christianity. They became known as *conversos*. Most conversos secretly maintained their Jewish faith and did not really accept Christian beliefs.

*Art showing Jews bowing down before Queen Isabella and her husband, King Ferdinand. Some Catholics have argued that Isabella should be made a saint, but many people disagree because of her treatment of the Jews and Muslims.*

In 1481, the Catholic ruler of Spain, Queen Isabella, set up an Inquisition. The people in charge of the Inquisition were given the power to decide if anyone was a **heretic.** Usually, few people were condemned for being a heretic, but many conversos were condemned because of their Jewish ancestry. They were said to be mixing in Jewish beliefs and practices with their practice of Catholicism. Those condemned were burned to death. Thousands of other conversos fled the country to avoid meeting the same fate.

In 1492, Queen Isabella ordered all Jews to leave the country. Those Jews who had not converted were forced to leave. They migrated to places such as Italy and Greece. Some reestablished Jewish communities in France and Germany that had been

## Interesting Fact

▸ Today, the Jewish population of Spain totals about 14,000.

abandoned during the Crusades. A few settled in the Netherlands. Jews from this last group eventually made their way to America.

Some Jews who were forced out of Spain and Portugal decided to settle in the Netherlands because the Dutch were relatively tolerant of different religions. The Dutch welcomed the Jews because of their great knowledge about trading. Many Sephardic Jews were experienced merchants. And because Jews were forced to migrate so many times throughout their history, they had relationships with other Jews all over the world. The Netherlands was not a country rich in natural resources. Its wealth was based mainly on trade. Dutch merchants wisely recognized that the Jews could help them do business because of these connections to other Jews.

In 1624, a small group of Dutch Jews joined a group of Dutch Christians and sailed to Brazil. They

*This painting shows the harbor of the city of Amsterdam in the Netherlands, during the 1600s. Amsterdam was a major center for trade during this period. Ships that left the port sailed all over the world, including faraway places such as Africa, North America, Indonesia, and Brazil.*

captured land from the Portuguese and established Dutch communities. By 1645, there were about 1,000 Jews living in Brazil. They built a synagogue in the town of Recife, the first one in the Americas. Then, in 1654, the Portuguese regained control of Recife. The Jews fled, fearing persecution.

Twenty-three Jews boarded a ship called the *Sainte Catherine.* It was sailing for the Dutch colony of New Amsterdam—known today as New York City. In September 1654, they stepped off the *Sainte Catherine* and set foot on what would become part of the United States. These 23 people were the first Jews who intended to make North America their home.

Over time, the Jewish population grew slowly and steadily. By 1700, about 200 Jews lived in North America. In 1820, almost 2,000 Jews lived in the United States. Then, in the early to middle 1800s, the pace of Jewish immigration to the United States began to pick up. There were several reasons for this.

At that time, Europe was undergoing an **industrial revolution.** More and more products were made in factories, and fewer and fewer were made by hand. Railroads were built that could carry goods quickly and easily from town to town—even from country to country. Many Jews had made their living as peddlers, selling goods from one town to another on foot or in horse-

▶ The first Jews in the United States were able to practice their faith even though there were no **rabbis** in North America. Services can be conducted by anyone with the knowledge to chant the prayers and read from the Torah (the first five books of the Bible).

*Peddlers did not have an easy job. Often traveling long distances to sell their goods, they had to watch out for thieves, accidents, and bad weather.*

drawn wagons. Modern transportation, however, made it easier to get farm goods to the cities and finished products made in cities back to people on farms. Peddlers were no longer needed. Some Jews with a little money settled in cities and opened factories or mills to produce goods. Some opened stores to sell goods produced by others. Many others, however, found themselves unable to make much of a living.

At the same time, Jews were hearing from people they knew in the United States that it was a good place to settle. While there was some **discrimination** against Jews in America, it was mild compared to what they had been subjected to in other parts of the world. So, many decided that their future was in the United States. By 1870, more than 200,000 Jews lived in the United States.

*A scene from one of the 200 pogroms that occurred in Russia in 1881. About 40 Jews were killed in the pogroms in Russia that year, and others were injured or had their homes and possessions destroyed. In many cases, the government and police did little to punish those responsible for this violent form of discrimination.*

Another reason that Jews were encouraged to come to the United States was the increase of pogroms—violent attacks on helpless people, in this case Jews. During bad economic times, Christians in Eastern Europe tended to blame Jews for their troubles. Some went so far as to attack and kill Jews. Many Jews came to America to escape this hatred.

In 1882, the May Laws were passed in Russia. These rules severely restricted the kind of work that Jews could do and where they could live. Already living at the lowest economic level of society, Jews sank further into poverty. The United States was seen as a place where they could make a better life.

## Interesting Fact

▶ Zur Israel was the name of the first synagogue built in the Americas. Its rabbi, Aboab da Fonseca, arrived in Recife in 1642 to lead the Jews. He was born in Portugal and educated in Amsterdam.

15

*As part of Hitler's plan to exterminate the Jews from Europe, the Nazis built prison camps during the 1930s and 1940s. The women and children shown in this photograph were prisoners at Auschwitz, a camp known for the huge number of Jews that were killed there.*

Large numbers of Jews continued to make their way to the United States until 1924. That year, the U.S. Congress passed strict laws limiting the number of immigrants entering the country. Few Jewish immigrants entered after that. During the late 1930s and early 1940s, Adolf Hitler, the leader of Nazi Germany, was ordering the extermination of European Jews. Even then, however, only about 150,000 Jews were allowed into the United States. By the end of World War II, more than 6 million European Jews had been murdered.

BAT MITZVAH MEANS "DAUGHTER OF THE COMMANDMENT." AT THE AGE OF 12 (age 13 for boys) Jewish children become obligated to observe the commandments of their religion. A bat mitzvah ceremony is a celebration of this milestone in a young Jewish woman's life. In 1922, no young woman in the United States had ever had a bat mitzvah ceremony. Only boys had been allowed to publicly celebrate this step to adulthood in bar mitzvah ceremonies.

Rabbi Mordecai M. Kaplan, the founder of Reconstructionist Judaism, believed that girls should also be honored with a celebration of this important event. So on Saturday, March 18, 1922, his daughter, Judith, celebrated her bat mitzvah in his synagogue. Today, it is common for Jewish girls to celebrate their bat mitzvahs, but back then, Judith Kaplan's bat mitzvah was considered shocking by many people.

Judith went on to become an accomplished musician. She married Ira Eisenstein, the assistant rabbi at her father's synagogue, in 1934. She taught music classes and eventually received a doctorate at the School of Sacred Music of Hebrew Union College. She created a radio series that broadcast a history of Jewish music, and she wrote the first book of American Jewish songs for children.

# Chapter THREE

# Becoming American

MOST OF THE EARLIEST JEWISH ARRIVALS LIVED ON the East Coast. Large Jewish American communities grew in New York, New York; Newport, Rhode Island; Savannah, Georgia; Charleston, South Carolina; and Philadelphia, Pennsylvania. Most Jews made their living as merchants. Many owned small stores. Those who were more successful **exported** raw mate-

*Jewish peddlers on Hester Street in Manhattan, New York, during the 1800s. Hester Street ran through an area that was home to many Jewish immigrants. The people who lived there faced overcrowded apartments, filthy living conditions, and a great deal of crime, but they were often grateful to have escaped the violent discrimination they suffered in Europe.*

*Construction began on the Touro Synagogue in 1759. In addition to being used as a hospital for British troops in 1776, a town meeting attended by George Washington was held there in 1781.*

rials from North America to Europe and **imported** finished products from Europe to the United States. Some of the richest Jewish Americans were involved in the slave trade.

As time went on and Jews began to believe that they were an accepted part of the community, they built synagogues and practiced their faith more openly. The Touro Synagogue in Newport, Rhode Island, is the oldest synagogue in the United States. It opened in 1763.

Jews have played a part in U.S. history since colonial times. When the Revolutionary War started, one of the first casualties was Francis Salvador, a Jew. Many other Jewish Americans fought in battles or helped the revolutionary cause in other ways. For instance, a Jewish doctor took care of General Washington's men at Valley Forge.

## Interesting Fact

▶ In 1776, during the Revolutionary War, the town of Newport, Rhode Island, was captured by the British. Most Jews left the city, and Touro Synagogue was used by the British troops as a hospital. In 1946, President Harry S. Truman proclaimed the synagogue to be a National Historic Site.

When the First Amendment to the U.S. Constitution became law, Jews were living in a country that guaranteed freedom of religion. But that didn't guarantee they would never experience discrimination again.

During the Civil War (1861–1865), Jews fought on both sides, North and South, depending on where they lived. Jews had lived in the United States since its founding and felt very much a part of their communities. But two events during the war reminded Jews that not all of their fellow citizens accepted their religion.

One of these was the passage of an act by Congress that said only Christian ministers could serve in the army. This meant that Jews would not have any rabbis serving them as chaplains. The second event occurred in 1862 when General Ulysses S. Grant said that all Jews in the region he commanded were to get out within 24 hours. Grant argued that Jews could not be trusted. This outraged leaders of the Jewish-American community. They arranged a meeting with President Lincoln. As soon as he learned of Grant's order, Lincoln overturned it.

By 1880, Jewish Americans were living in almost every state. Most Jewish immigrants arrived in New York City. It was common for a man and his children who were old enough to make a living to come to America first. They would settle in,

*Chickens hang in the window of a kosher butcher shop in the United States during the 1930s. Kosher is the Yiddish word for proper. Food that is kosher has been prepared according to the dietary laws followed by those who practice the Jewish faith.*

usually with the help of a relative or friend who had immigrated earlier, and begin to work and save money. When they had enough money saved, they would send for the mother and younger children to join them.

By 1905, nearly 700,000 Jews were living in New York City. Other large Jewish-American communities could be found in Chicago, Illinois, (with about 80,000 Jews) and Philadelphia, Pennsylvania (home to about 75,000 Jews). In these Jewish communities, particularly in New York City, a rich Jewish cultural and social life developed.

Some Jews opened shops that sold goods to other Jews. Because the practice of Judaism requires following certain laws about food and how it is prepared, kosher butcher shops, bakeries, food stores, and restaurants were opened to serve the community. These shops employed many Jews and helped everyone preserve their Jewish heritage. Kosher shops can still be found in Jewish-American neighborhoods today.

A large number of Jewish immigrants went to work in the garment industry. Many Jews were seamstresses and tailors in Europe. They found they could use those skills to make a living in America. Most of the owners of the clothing factories were Jewish as well. Conditions in some of these factories were terrible. People—many of them women and children—worked long hours for low wages. It is not surprising, then, that some of the people who helped create the American labor movement were Jewish-American women. Some of the most famous among them were Pauline Newman, Bessie Abramowitz, and Rose Schneiderman.

Samuel Gompers was also involved in the labor movement. He took a job in a cigar shop when he arrived in New York. He joined the Cigar Makers' National Union. He eventually went on to help create the American Federation of Labor (AFL).

Louis Brandeis was an attorney who was educated at Harvard University. He was the first Jew to be nominated to the U.S. Supreme Court. His nomination in 1916 stirred up much debate over whether or not it was appropriate for a Jew to sit on the Supreme Court of a country in which most citizens were Christian. Despite the **anti-Semitic** views of many members of Congress and U.S. society, his nomination was approved after months of heated debate.

*When Louis Brandeis served on the U.S. Supreme Court, one of the other justices discriminated against Jews and refused to sit next to him during meetings.*

Anti-Semitism has never been completely wiped out in the United States. During the 1930s, at the height of the Great Depression, prejudice against Jews ran high. This didn't stop Hank Greenberg, a famous baseball player with the Detroit Tigers, from calling attention to his Jewish heritage. In September 1934, his team was scheduled to play on Yom Kippur, a very important religious holiday for Jews. Greenberg refused to play on that day, even though his team was trying hard to capture the American League pennant. Greenberg, a star of

▶ Many young Jewish garment workers died in the Triangle Shirtwaist Company fire on March 25, 1911. Most were young women between the ages of 13 and 23. When fire broke out, many of the workers were unable to escape because the owners of the factory had locked the doors to the exits. Of the company's 500 workers, 146 died in the fire. It was the worst factory fire in New York history.

the sport that many people consider to be a symbol of the United States, managed to also remain faithful to his Jewish heritage.

In 1947, a Jewish American came to symbolize America to people around the world when Bess Meyerson won the Miss America pageant. Today, Jewish Americans can be found in every state of the union and in all professions. When those 23 Jews set foot on American soil in 1654, they had no idea that they were starting what would one day become the largest Jewish community in the world.

*Hank Greenberg during a baseball training exercise in 1937. In 1956, Greenberg became the first Jewish player elected to the Baseball Hall of Fame.*

MANY PEOPLE ARE AWARE that Jews were very involved in the development of the garment industry in the United States. But did you know that Jewish Americans also played a leading role in the creation of the movie industry?

Adolph Zukor, a Hungarian immigrant, founded the Famous Players Film Company in 1912. The next year, he invested in a film distribution company called Paramount Pictures. Carl Laemmle, a Jewish immigrant from Germany, founded Universal Studios. Samuel Goldwyn, born in Warsaw, Poland, started Goldwyn Pictures. His company became part of Metro-Goldwyn-Mayer (MGM), which was run by another Jewish American, Louis Mayer. Four Jewish brothers from Poland—Sam, Harry, Jack, and Albert Warner—started Warner Brothers Studios.

Ever since the Hollywood film industry started, Jewish Americans have held many of its top jobs. Today, Sherry Lansing (above) runs Paramount Motion Pictures, Harvey Weinstein heads the Miramax Film Corporation, and Michael Eisner is the chairman and CEO of Walt Disney Productions.

# Chapter FOUR

# Famous Jewish Americans

*Albert Einstein on his 70th birthday in 1949, surrounded by Jewish children who were forced to flee Europe to escape Hitler's persecution. Einstein gave up his German citizenship and immigrated to the United States in response to Hitler's persecution of the Jews.*

TODAY, THE UNITED STATES IS HOME TO MORE JEWS than any other country in the world. Its Jewish-American citizens have made lasting contributions in every field.

Jonas Salk and Albert Sabin are two of the most famous American physicians of the 20th century. In the first half of the 1900s, polio was a disease feared by many. They invented two different vaccines that are still used to prevent polio today.

Maybe the most famous Jewish-American scientist is Albert Einstein. Born in Germany, he came to the United States in 1933 and gave up his German citizenship in response to Hitler's hatred and perse-

cution of the Jews. Einstein won the Nobel Prize in physics in 1921.

Hank Greenberg was not the only famous Jewish-American athlete. Sandy Koufax pitched for the Dodgers. He followed in Greenberg's footsteps when he refused to pitch in the 1965 World Series on Yom Kippur. Koufax and Greenberg are the only two Jewish Americans to have been elected to the Baseball Hall of Fame.

In 1985, Senda Berenson was the first woman elected to the Basketball Hall of Fame. A teacher at Smith College, she introduced a women's version of the game in 1892. Other famous Jewish-American athletes include Olympic gold medal winners Mark Spitz and Mitch Gaylord.

Novelist Judy Blume has written many popular books for young people. *Superfudge, Blubber,* and *Forever* are just a few of the titles that have made this Jewish-American author famous.

Jewish-American musicians include Leonard Bernstein, Richard Rodgers, Oscar Hammerstein, and George Gershwin. Jewish-American composer Irving Berlin wrote the song "God Bless America."

There are many famous entertainers who are Jewish Americans. Actors Nathan Lane and Matthew Broderick played Jewish-American characters in the zany Mel Brooks musical *The Producers.* Brooks is one of the greatest Jewish-American comedians of all time. Steven Spielberg has directed

▶ Sandy Koufax excelled at more than just baseball. He was awarded a basketball scholarship to attend the University of Cincinnati.

many exciting movies, including *Jaws, Raiders of the Lost Ark,* and *Jurassic Park.* Richard Dreyfus, Natalie Portman, Barbra Streisand, Jerry Seinfeld, and Goldie Hawn are just a few of the Jewish Americans who entertain people around the world.

Many U.S. government leaders have been Jewish Americans. Today, Ruth Bader Ginsburg and Stephen Breyer sit on the U.S. Supreme Court. Senator Joseph Lieberman from Connecticut was the Democratic Party's vice presidential candidate in the 2000 election.

Jewish Americans have been part of the United States since its beginning. Their contributions have helped make America what it is today. As the 21st century unfolds, they continue to honor their Jewish heritage and religious customs while being proud citizens of the United States of America.

*At the Tony Awards ceremony in 2001, Mel Brooks (left) hugs Nathan Lane (center) while co-star Matthew Broderick (right) watches. They were celebrating the 12 Tony Awards won by* The Producers *that year.*

28

**1492**     **1933**     **1934**

**586 B.C.**   Jews are forced into exile in Babylonia.

**536**   Jews return to their homeland and rebuild their temple.

**A.D. 70**   The Romans begin forcing the Jews out of their homeland again.

**1095**   The first of the Crusades begins, and Christian soldiers murder many Jews on their way to Jerusalem.

**1481**   The Inquisition begins in Spain and many Jews are killed, while others begin leaving the country.

**1492**   Queen Isabella orders all Jews out of Spain.

**1654**   The Portuguese take control of Recife in Brazil; Jews flee Brazil, and 23 of them arrive in New Amsterdam.

**1700**   The population of Jews in North America is about 200.

**1763**   The Touro Synagogue in Newport, Rhode Island, is formally opened.

**1862**   General Ulysses S. Grant orders all Jews under his command to leave the region.

**1870**   The population of Jewish Americans reaches 200,000.

**1905**   The population of Jews in New York City nears 700,000.

**1916**   Louis Brandeis becomes the first Jewish-American justice of the U.S. Supreme Court.

**1933**   Adolf Hitler takes control of Germany and begins his systematic murder of millions of European Jews; Albert Einstein immigrates to the United States and gives up his German citizenship.

**1934**   Hank Greenberg refuses to play baseball on Yom Kippur.

**1947**   Bess Meyerson is crowned Miss America.

**1965**   Sandy Koufax refuses to play in the World Series on Yom Kippur.

**1976**   Milton Friedman wins the Nobel Prize in economics.

**1985**   Senda Berenson becomes the first woman elected to the Basketball Hall of Fame.

**2000**   Senator Joseph Lieberman of Connecticut runs for vice president of the United States on the Democratic Party ticket.

**anti-Semitic (an-ti-seh-MIH-tik)**
Someone who is anti-Semitic discriminates against Jews. Some people in the United States have anti-Semitic viewpoints.

**Crusaders (kroo-SADE-ers)**
Crusaders were Christian soldiers who tried to take biblical lands away from the Muslims who controlled them in the 11th, 12th, and 13th centuries. The Crusaders killed many Jews as they made their way to Jerusalem.

**discrimination (dis-KRI-meh-NA-shun)**
Discrimination is the practice of treating certain groups of people unfairly or un-equally because of an unreasonable dislike or distrust of them. Discrimination against Jews in America was usually mild compared to what they were subjected to in other parts of the world.

**exported (ek-SPORT-ed)**
If something is exported, it is sent to another country to be sold there. Some Jews exported raw materials from North America to other countries.

**heretic (HER-uh-tik)**
A heretic is someone whose views are not acceptable to the leaders of a particular religious group. The people in charge of the Inquisition were given the power to determine if anyone was a heretic.

**imported (im-PORT-ed)**
Something that is imported is brought into a country from somewhere else. Some Jews imported finished goods from Europe and sold them in the United States.

**industrial revolution (in-DUHSS-tree-uhl rev-uh-LOO-shuhn)**
The industrial revolution is the period in history during which the economy changed over from one dominated by farming and handcrafts to one based mainly on the production of goods by machines. Many Jews migrated to the United States when Europe was in the middle of the industrial revolution.

**Inquisition (in-kweh-ZIH-shun)**
The Inquisition was a formal group set up by the Roman Catholic Church to investigate those deemed to be unfaithful. In 1481, Queen Isabella of Spain ordered the beginning of the Spanish Inquisition.

**rabbis (RAB-eyes)**
Rabbis are Jewish religious leaders and teachers. During the Civil War, rabbis were not allowed to serve as chaplains in the armed forces.

# For Further INFORMATION

## Web Sites

Visit our homepage for lots of links about Jewish Americans:
**http://www.childsworld.com/links.html**

*Note to Parents, Teachers, and Librarians:*
We routinely verify our Web links to make sure they're safe,
active sites—so encourage your readers to check them out!

## Books

Brooks, Philip. *Extraordinary Jewish Americans.* Danbury, Conn.:
Children's Press, 1998.

Senker, Cath. *Judaism.* Columbus, Ohio: Peter Bedrick Books, 2002.

Stein, Robert. *Jewish Americans.* Hauppage, N.Y.: Barron's Educational Series, 2003.

## Places to Visit or Contact

### Touro Synagogue
*To tour the oldest synagogue in North America*
85 Touro Street
Newport, RI 02840
401/847-4794

### Spertus Museum
*To learn more about Jewish history, religion, and culture*
618 South Michigan Avenue
Chicago, IL 60605
312/322-1747

# Index

## About the Author

PAM ROSENBERG IS A FORMER JUNIOR HIGH SCHOOL TEACHER AND corporate trainer. She currently works as an author and editor of children's books. She has always loved reading and feels very fortunate to be doing work that requires her to read all the time. When she isn't writing or editing books she enjoys spending time with her husband and two children and reading just for fun. She lives in Chicago.